Animals That Live in the Forest/
Animales del bosque

Black Bears/
Osos negros

By JoAnn Early Macken

Reading Consultant: Jeanne Clidas, Ph.D.
Director, Roberts Wesleyan College Literacy Clinic

WEEKLY READER®
PUBLISHING

Please visit our web site at **www.garethstevens**
For a free catalog describing our list of high-qu
call 1-877-542-2595 (USA) or 1-800-387-3178 (C
Our fax: 1-877-542-2596

Library of Congress Cataloging-in-Publication

Macken, JoAnn Early, 1953–
   [Black bears. Spanish & English]
   Black bears = Osos negros / by JoAnn
     p. cm. — (Animals that live in the fo
   Includes bibliographical references and index.
   English and Spanish; translated from the English.
   ISBN-10: 1-4339-2434-X   ISBN-13: 978-1-4339-2434-7 (lib. bdg.)
   ISBN-10: 1-4339-2485-4   ISBN-13: 978-1-4339-2485-9 (soft cover)
   1. Black bear—Juvenile literature. I. Title. II. Title: Osos negros.
   QL737.C27M23718   2009
   599.78'5—dc22

                                  2009008339

This edition first published in 2010 by
Weekly Reader® Books
An Imprint of Gareth Stevens Publishing
1 Reader's Digest Road
Pleasantville, NY 10570-7000 USA

Copyright © 2010 by Gareth Stevens, Inc.

Executive Managing Editor: Lisa M. Herrington
Senior Editor: Barbara Bakowski
Cover Designers: Jennifer Ryder-Talbot and Studio Montage
Production: Studio Montage
Translators: Tatiana Acosta and Guillermo Gutiérrez
Library Consultant: Carl Harvey, Library Media Specialist, Noblesville, Indiana

Photo credits: Cover, pp. 1, 11, 13 Shutterstock; p. 5 © Lisa and Mike Husar/TeamHusar.com; p. 7 © Tom Ulrich/
Visuals Unlimited; p. 9 © Alan and Sandy Carey; pp. 15, 19 © Tom and Pat Leeson; p. 17 © Michael H. Francis;
p. 21 © Dave Welling

Printed in the United States of America

1 2 3 4 5 6 7 8 9 14 13 12 11 10 09

¿Qué me dice el contenido?

Table of Contents

Contenido

Boldface words appear in the glossary./
Las palabras en **negrita** aparecen en el glosario.

Asleep in a Den

A hungry bear **cub** cries. Its mother holds the baby close and feeds it milk. Then she goes back to sleep.

- - - - - - - - - - -

Dormidos en la madriguera

Un **osezno** hambriento llora. Su madre se lo acerca y lo alimenta con su leche. Después, vuelve a dormirse.

cubs/
oseznos

Black bears **hibernate**, or sleep, during the cold winter. They live on their fat until the weather turns warm.

– – – – – – – – – – –

Los osos negros **hibernan**, o duermen, durante el frío invierno. Hasta que llega el buen tiempo, viven de la grasa de su cuerpo.

Finding Food

In spring, black bears wake up and search for food. At first, they find green **shoots** of plants. Later, bears look for nuts and berries.

– – – – – – – – – –

En busca de comida

En primavera, los osos negros despiertan y salen en busca de comida. Primero descubren los verdes **brotes** de las plantas. Después, buscan frutos secos y bayas.

Black bears also eat small animals and insects. They look for insects under rocks and logs. They dig with their **claws**.

Los osos negros también comen insectos y otros animales pequeños. Buscan insectos debajo de rocas y troncos, escarbando con las **garras**.

Black bears find food by smell. This bear has caught a fish! Bears must eat a lot in spring and summer. They must put on fat for the winter.

– – – – – – – – – – – –

Los osos negros usan el olfato para encontrar comida. ¡Este oso ha atrapado un pez! Los osos deben comer mucho en primavera y verano. Tienen que acumular grasa para el invierno.

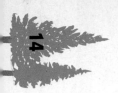

A Bear's Life

Black bears have soft, thick fur. Not all black bears are black! Some are brown. Others are lighter colors.

La vida de un oso

Los osos negros tienen un pelaje suave y denso. ¡No todos los osos negros son de color negro! Algunos tienen el pelaje marrón o de colores más claros.

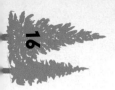

Black bears walk flat on their feet, just as people do. The bears can run faster than people can.

– – – – – – – – – –

Los osos negros caminan erguidos sobre las patas, como las personas. Los osos pueden correr más rápido que una persona.

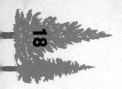

Young cubs stay with their mothers. When danger is near, a mother bear sends her cub up a tree. The cub is safer there.

- - - - - - - - - - - -

Los oseznos se quedan con su madre. Si hay algún peligro, la osa pone al osezno en un árbol. Allí el osezno está más seguro.

Some bears **gather** where there is plenty of food. Most bears spend their days alone.

- - - - - - - - - - -

Algunos osos se **concentran** en lugares donde abunda la comida. La mayoría de los osos viven solos.

Fast Facts/Datos básicos

Height/Altura	about 3 feet (1 meter) at the shoulder/ unos 3 pies (1 metros) en la cruz
Length/Longitud	about 7 feet (2 meters) nose to tail/ unos 7 pies (2 metros) de nariz a cola
Weight/Peso	Males: about 500 pounds (227 kilograms)/ Machos: unas 500 libras (227 kilogramos) Females: about 300 pounds (136 kilograms)/ Hembras: unas 300 libras (136 kilogramos)
Diet/Dieta	nuts, fruit, insects, fish, meat, and greens/ frutos secos, fruta, insectos, peces, carne y vegetales
Average life span/Promedio de vida	up to 34 years/ hasta 34 años

Glossary/Glosario

claws: sharp, curved nails on an animal's foot

cub: a baby bear or other animal

gather: to meet

hibernate: to go into a deep sleep for a long time

shoots: the new growth of green plants

– – – – – – – – –

brotes: tallos nuevos de las plantas

concentrarse: reunirse

garras: uñas afiladas

hibernar: permanecer en un sueño profundo durante mucho tiempo

osezno: cría de oso

For More Information/Más información

Books/Libros

Bears/Los osos. Animals I See at the Zoo (series).
JoAnn Early Macken (Gareth Stevens, 2003)

Bears/Osos. Baby Animals (series). Alice Twine
(Rosen Publishing Group, 2008)

Web Sites/Páginas web

Black Bears/Osos negros

www.bear-tracker.com/bear.html

See paw prints and claw marks. Hear a bear roar, too!/
Miren huellas de oso y marcas de sus garras. ¡También pueden
oír el rugido de un oso!

North American Bear Center/Centro norteamericano del oso

www.bear.org

Tune in to see images from a webcam outside a den./Vean
imágenes desde una webcam situada junto a una madriguera.

Index/Índice

claws 10	food 4, 8, 10, 12, 20	sleeping 4, 6
cubs 4, 18	fur 14	walking 16
danger 18	hibernating 4, 6	
feet 16	running 16	

- - - - - - - - - - - - -

caminar 16	dormir 4, 6	patas 16
comida 4, 8, 10, 12, 20	garras 10	pelaje 14
correr 16	hibernación 4, 6	peligro 18
	oseznos 4, 18	

About the Author

JoAnn Early Macken is the author of two rhyming picture books, *Sing-Along Song* and *Cats on Judy*, and more than 80 nonfiction books for children. Her poems have appeared in several children's magazines. She lives in Wisconsin with her husband and their two sons.

- - - - - - - - - - - - -

Información sobre la autora

JoAnn Early Macken ha escrito dos libros de rimas con ilustraciones, *Sing-Along Song* y *Cats on Judy*, y más de ochenta libros de no ficción para niños. Sus poemas han sido publicados en varias revistas infantiles. Vive en Wisconsin con su esposo y sus dos hijos.